Viols, Violins and Virginals

Jennifer A. Charlton

THE HILL COLLECTION
OF STRINGED INSTRUMENTS
AT THE
ASHMOLEAN MUSEUM, OXFORD

OTHER ILLUSTRATED BOOKS

The Finzi Bowl (Lawrence Whistler)
Three Sonnets by Raphael
Toy Soldiers and ceremonial in Post-Mughal India
The Forest Fire of Piero di Cosimo
T. E. Lawrence: Lawrence of Arabia
Ark to Ashmolean – The story of the Tradescants and
                the Ashmolean Museum

Cover illustration: Detail from a 17th century needlework
                hanging of A Musical Party

Designed by Andrew Ivett. Set in Palatino and printed in
Great Britain by the Holywell Press Ltd., Oxford 1985.
Reprinted 1999.

Introduction

The Hill Collection of Musical Instruments is one of the world's most outstanding collections of European stringed instruments. The Hill Music Room was opened in 1950 to house the collection, originally presented to the Museum in 1939 by Messrs Alfred and Arthur Hill, partners in the reknowned firm of W. E. Hill and Sons, followed in 1946 and 1948 by supplementary gifts from Mr. A. Phillips Hill. The Collection was further extended in 1999 by the gift of additional instruments and bows from Mr. Albert Cooper.

This small booklet contains a brief outline of the development of the various instruments. More detailed descriptions of the individual instruments in the collection can be found in the Catalogue of the Collection by Professor David R. Boyden of the University of California at Berkeley. The booklet is divided as follows –

> Bowed Instruments: *Viols and Violins*
> Bows
> Plucked Instruments: *Citterns and Guitars*
> Keyboard Instruments: *Harpsichords and Virginals*

Each section is illustrated with photographs of selected instruments from the collection, all of which came to the museum as gifts from Hills, with the exception of the Stainer Violin (Pl. 10) and the Kirckman Harpsichord (Pl. 22).

Within the University of Oxford other collections of musical instruments may be seen at the PITT RIVERS MUSEUM, Parks Road and Banbury Road (Mondays to Saturdays 1 – 4.30) and THE BATE COLLECTION OF HISTORICAL (WIND) INSTRUMENTS, at the FACULTY OF MUSIC, St. Aldate's (Mondays to Fridays 2 – 5 and Saturdays in Full-Term 10 – 12).

Bowed Instruments: *Viols and Violins*

It was not until the fifteenth century that instrumental music came to be regarded as being of importance in itself. Previously, with the exception of 'dance' music composed for the 'vielle' or 'fiede', music had been restricted to voices and the only important music – Church music.

During the fifteenth century instrumental music was developed, at first combined with and later substituted for, voices. The organ and domestic instruments such as lutes, citterns, viols, recorders and keyboard instruments were rapidly gaining popularity.

Viols were developed from the medieval vielle, held in front of the body and not under the chin like the violin. They were flat backed, with sloping shoulders, and six strings. The finger-boards were fretted and the bridge more arched than the violin. They had 'C' shaped sound holes and usually an ornamented head. The hand was held under the bow and not above as for the violin.

Viols came in various sizes but were chiefly designed to play the upper, lower and inner parts of a composition. A 'chest of viols' which was literally a box fitted for holding these instruments usually consisted of two trebles, two tenors (or one alto and one tenor) and two basses. Music was then composed for a 'consort of viols'.

The bass viol which is the most important member of the viol group (unlike the violin family) is called the 'Viola da gamba' and comes from a large family of instruments which are played together either resting on the knees or between them ('gamba' from the Italian meaning leg).

The Hill Collection also contains two small bass 'lyra' viols. They were tuned in a similar manner to the Lira da Braccio (which is described below), to facilitate the playing of chords – a mixture of 4ths and 5ths. The tuning was variable and was marked at the beginning of each piece of music.

Violins did not evolve from viols as is often imagined, but developed alongside them. It was not until the latter part of the seventeenth century that violins took precedence over viols, 'though the more popular 'viola da gamba' continued nearly to the end of the eighteenth century and in recent years has been revived.

One of the principal ancestors of the violin was the Lira da Braccio, familiar from representations of 'Heavenly choirs' in renaissance art, but which had virtually passed out of use by 1550. These instruments, designed to be played on the arm, had wide fingerboards with five strings and two 'Bourdon' or drone strings which were not stopped by the fingers, running off the fingerboard. A feature which can clearly be seen in plate six. This instrument already has features of the violin – f-shaped sound holes and the bowed back.

The home of the violin is Northern Italy, and the great violin making families of Amati, Guarneri and Stradivari in Cremona from the mid sixteenth to the eighteenth century, brought the instrument to the height of perfection. At this time the pitch was somewhat lower than nowadays and numerous old instruments have been damaged by the increased tension of the strings.

In addition to bowed backs and 'f' shaped sound holes, violins have four strings tuned in 5ths. The fingerboard is without frets and the bow is held overhand.

The family consists of violin, viola (both held under chin); 'cello and double bass, resting by means of a 'peg' on the floor.

In addition to the world-famous 'Le Messie' Stradivarius violin, the Ashmolean collection includes the 'Alard' violin made by Nicola Amati in Cremona in 1649; together with a tenor viola and a small violin (one of the oldest in existence) both made by Andrea Amati for Charles IX of France, in 1574 and 1564 respectively.

1. Treble Viol by Giovanni Maria of Brescia, made in Venice, probably between 1500 and 1525. One of the oldest treble Viols still extant.

2. Bass Viol by Gasparo da Salò, Brescia. Late sixteenth century.

3. Bass Viol – some-
times called the
'Beaufort Viol' –
attributed to John Rose
of Bridewell, London,
c.1600.

4. Small Bass (Lyra) Viol
by John Rose, London,
1598.

5. Bass Viol with certain features of a 'Cello by the 'Brothers Amati' – Antonius and Hieronymus, sons of Andrea Amati, Cremona, 1611. Once in the collection of the Medici.

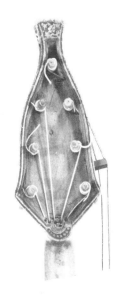

6. Seven-stringed Lira da Braccio – one of the ancestors of the Violin – by Giovanni Maria of Brescia, Venice, *c*.1525. The detail shows the reverse rather than the front of the pegbox.

7. 'Charles IX' Violin by Andrea Amati, Cremona, 1564. One of thirty-eight stringed instruments commissioned for the Court from Amati. Slightly smaller than a modern instrument.

8. 'Charles IX' larger tenor Viola by Andrea Amati, Cremona, 1574.

9. 'Alard' Violin by Nicola Amati, grandson of Andrea, Cremona, 1649. Once in the possession of Delphin Alard the Violinist (1811-88).

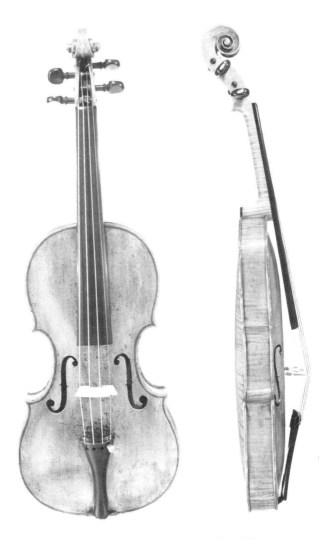

10. Violin by Jacob Stainer, Absam in Tyrol, 1672.

11. Inlaid Violin, possibly for a child, by Antonio Stradivari, Cremona, 1683.

12. 'Le Messie' Violin –
possibly the most
famous violin in the
world – by Antonio
Stradivari, Cremona,
1716.

Bows

The Bow, from its earliest development, has undergone considerable changes to its present day shape.

The first bows were convex and resembled the archer's bow, hence the name, but gradually the curve became less defined, though still convex, until the end of the eighteenth century. This type of bow had advantages for playing seventeenth century music (especially the music of the Bach era) on viols, as it was less springy than the modern bow, with less likelihood of the stick being forced upon the string by the pressure of chord playing.

The modern bow with its 'concave' stick developed at the hands of François Tourte (1747 – 1835). As well as being concave it has been increased in length and weight. It is more springy for spiccato and orchestral playing.

Most of the bows in the Ashmolean are English, from the mid-late eighteenth century, but they include one by François Tourte's father, made *c.*1760.

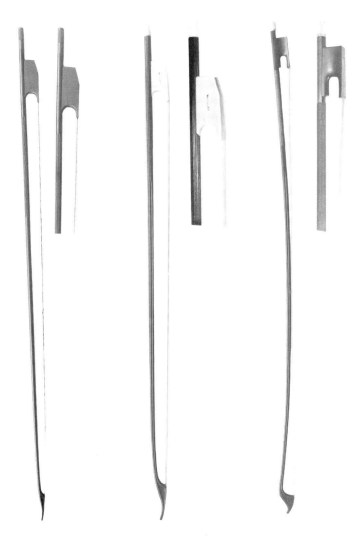

13. (from left) Violin Bow, *c*.1700; Bass-Viol Bow by Peter Walmsley (1720/40); Violin Bow by Tourte Père, the father of François Tourte, *c*.1760.

Plucked Instruments: *Citterns and Guitars*

The guitar seems to have originated and developed in Spain and Italy and its origins go back to antiquity. The instrument is similar to the lute, with a fretted fingerboard. The back however is flat, the resonance chamber is deep-ribbed, more like a violin, and the earlier instruments were double-strung like lutes. The Collection does however include an elaborately inlaid Venetian *chitarra battente*, differing in shape from the true guitar, and with a rounded back.

It is most likely that the guitar developed from the Spanish vihuela de mano. Both the vihuela and lute were instruments of the aristocracy whereas the guitar enjoyed more popular favour, being both less expensive to make and easier to play – because of its stringing and tuning. Its popularity soon spread to France and England during the sixteenth century. On his death in 1547 Henry VIII was found to have had twenty one guitars in his collection of three hundred and eighty one instruments. A particular rarity to be found in the Hill Collection is a Stradivarius guitar, made in Cremona in 1688.

The cittern is thought to have developed from the medieval citole, and enjoyed much popularity in the sixteenth and seventeenth centuries. Viewed from the front it was similar to the lute, though more circular, and flat backed like a guitar. Like the guitar it too was less expensive to make and its wire strings made it quite bright and suitable for popular tunes, often being referred to as 'the poor man's lute'. Indeed citterns were often provided in barbers' shops for the amusement of waiting customers. In the early eighteenth century the instrument went into decline and was superseded by the 'English guitar' which had a slightly different shape with a larger body and deeper ribs. These instruments, of which there are five in the Hill Collection, went out of fashion about 1800.

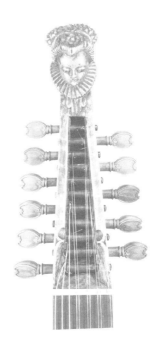

14. Cittern by Gasparo da Salo, Brescia, *c*.1560.

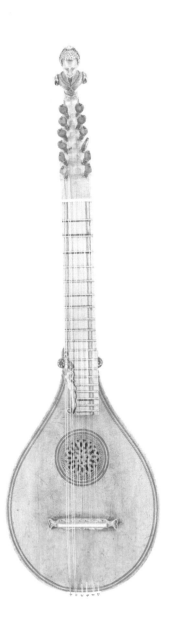

15. Italian
seventeenth-century
Cittern.

16. English Guitar with watch-key tuning, by J.N. Preston, London, *c.*1734/70.

17. English Guitar with tuning pegs, by J.N. Preston, London, *c*.1734/70.

18. Chitarra Battente Guitar (to be played with plectrum) –
probably descended from the old 'Vihuela de penola' – by Giorgio
Sellas, Venice, 1627.

19. Guitar by René Voboam, French School, 1641.

20. Guitar by Antonio Stradivari, Cremona, 1688 (or possibly 1680) – very plain in its appearance, but nonetheless a most beautifully designed instrument.

Keyboard Instruments:
Harpsichords and Virginals

The harpsichord was the most popular of the major domestic instruments – harpsichord, virginal, spinet and clavichord. It represented the highest state of the development of plucked keyboard instruments and was the basis for most of the chamber music written between 1600 and 1800.

Harpsichords, spinets and virginals differ from the clavichord and piano in that the strings are *plucked* not *struck*. The harpsichord family is therefore more likely to have been derived from the psaltery and the clavichord and piano from the dulcimer.

The harpsichord in its basic form has the strings set at right angles to the keyboard. The keys on being played lift a 'jack' which in turn has a 'plectrum', or 'quill', or piece of leather attached, which 'plucks' the string in passing. The 'jack' then falls back into position without touching the string. In the more advanced forms of the instrument there are more sets of strings, often an octave higher, or less frequently, an octave lower than the basic string. Sometimes these strings are worked from the same manual, or keyboard, but sometimes a second manual is added. The number of strings used to a note could be varied by mechanical means, i.e. by pulling out stops, as in organ playing, or by using pedals. These stops or pedals brought into, or put out of, action new strings, varying the tonal quality. This had not previously been possible because finger pressure, so important in piano playing, had little influence on the sound produced. Frequent tuning was essential for the harpsichord owing mainly to the thinness and length of the strings and also frequent 're-quilling' was necessary. Probably this was one of the causes, along with lack of tonal range, that led to its decline in favour of the piano.

Virginals were the earliest and simplest form of the harpsichord. The strings, running from right to left, and parallel to the keyboard, were housed in a box which varied in size and which was intended to be placed on a table or sometimes set on legs.

The origin of the name virginals is obscure, but it is thought that it was originally an instrument to be played by young ladies. A theory supported by the fact that the first music printed for the instrument was called *Parthenia*, i.e. *Maiden's Songs*.

The Hill Collection contains both a harpsichord and a virginal. Both English, the former by the famous Jacob Kirckman (1710-92), was presented to the museum by Mrs Bowman in 1948, and the latter, by Adam Leversidge, came to the museum as part of the original Hill Gift.

21. Virginal with a compass of four and a half octaves, by Adam Leversidge, London, 1670.

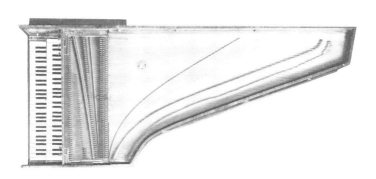

22. Two-manual Harpsichord by Jacob Kirckman, London, 1772.

Guide to Further Reading

Grove's Dictionary of Music
The New Oxford History of Music Vol. 4.
Musical Instruments through the Ages ed. Buchner
Musical Instruments through the Ages ed. Anthony Baines
Musical Instruments Sybil Marcuse
Old Musical Instruments Rene Clemenicic
Hamlyn Colour Encyclopaedia of Musical Instruments
    Alexander Buchner, trsl. S. Pellar
European Musical Instruments Frank Harrison & Joan Rimmer
History of Musical Instuments Curt Sachs
An Encyclopaedia of the Violin Bachmann
The Amadeus Book of the Violin Walter Kolneder
The Violin Family (New Grove Musical Instruments Series)
The Violin Family and its makers in the British Isles B. W. Harvey
Universal Dictionary of the Violin and Bow Makers William Henley
Bows and Bow Makers William C. Retford
Early History of the Viol Ian Woodfield
Illustrated History of the Guitar Alexander Bellow
The Guitar from Renaissance to Present Day Harvey Turnbull
Early Keyboard Instruments Philip Kames
Keyboard Instruments 1500-1800 ed. Edwin M. Ripin

For the Younger Reader

The Wonderful World of Music
    Benjamin Britten and Imogen Holst
The First Book of Music Gertrude Norman
The Story of Music Geoffrey Brace (Ladybird Books)
Oxford Junior Companion to Music ed. Percy A. Scholes
Instruments of the Orchestra (Young Reader's guide to music
    Vol. 4) Mervyn Bruxner
Instruments of the Orchestra (Cambridge assignments in music)
    Ray Bennett
Musical Instruments Denys Davlow
*The Orchestra – an illustrated guide to the history and development of
    instruments and music* Michael Hurd
Oxford first companion to instruments and orchestras
    Kenneth and Valerie McLeish